DINO DUEL

T. REX VS. ANKYLOSAURUS

Prehistoric Showdown

Tom Jackson

Lerner Publications ◆ Minneapolis

Lerner Publications Company
An imprint of Lerner Publishing Group, Inc.
241 First Avenue North
Minneapolis, MN 55401 USA

For reading levels and more information, look up this title at www.lernerbooks.com.

Main body text set in Aptifer Sans LT Pro.
Typeface provided by Linotype.

Library of Congress Cataloging-in-Publication Data

Names: Jackson, Tom, 1972–author.
Title: T. Rex vs. Ankylosaurus : prehistoric showdown / Tom Jackson.
Description: Minneapolis : Lerner Publications , [2026] | Series: Dino duel | Includes bibliographical references and index. | Audience: Ages 8–11 | Audience: Grades 4–6 | Summary: "The T. Rex might be large and speedy, but the ankylosaurus has thick, armored skin. Read about these dinosaurs and who might come out on top in a fight"—Provided by publisher.
Identifiers: LCCN 2024047643 (print) | LCCN 2024047644 (ebook) | ISBN 9798765669259 (lib. bdg.) | ISBN 9798765683927 (pbk.) | ISBN 9798765676738 (epub)
Subjects: LCSH: Tyrannosaurus rex—Juvenile literature. | Ankylosaurus—Juvenile literature.
Classification: LCC QE862.S3 J332 2026 (print) | LCC QE862.S3 (ebook) | DDC 567.912/9—dc23/eng/20250123

LC record available at https://lccn.loc.gov/2024047643
LC ebook record available at https://lccn.loc.gov/2024047644

Manufactured in the United States of America
1 – CG – 7/15/25

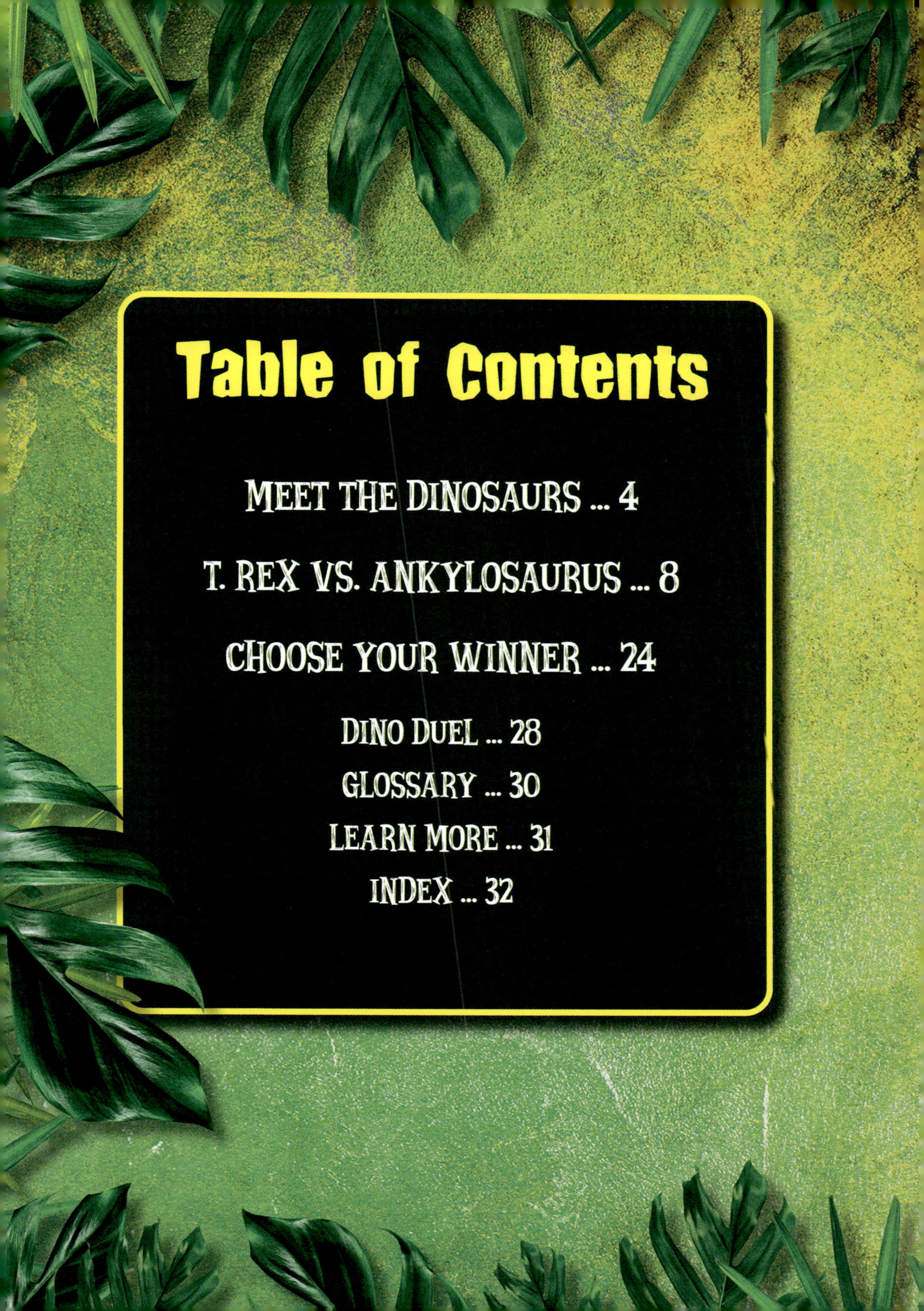

Table of Contents

MEET THE DINOSAURS ... 4

T. REX VS. ANKYLOSAURUS ... 8

CHOOSE YOUR WINNER ... 24

DINO DUEL ... 28

GLOSSARY ... 30

LEARN MORE ... 31

INDEX ... 32

MEET THE DINOSAURS

The T. rex is on the move.

A hungry T. rex stomps through a forest. The forest is quiet, but the T. rex knows where it might find some food. It can smell an animal nearby. The giant predator follows the scent. It walks slowly and quietly through the bushes. Soon it can see its next prey through the leaves. It is an ankylosaurus.

The ankylosaurus is also hungry, even though it has been grazing on leaves for most of the day. It can smell the tasty plants all around it. But there is another smell. What is it? Just as the ankylosaurus looks up, the T. rex charges out of the bush. Its huge teeth are easy to see in its open mouth.

The ankylosaurus senses danger!

The two mighty dinosaurs get ready to fight.

The ankylosaurus does not run away. It cannot move faster than the big hunter in front of it. However, it can defend against an attack from this T. rex. It has thick skin armored with bone plates. Even a T. rex will find it hard to bite into those. And the ankylosaurus has a weapon to fight back with.

The end of the ankylosaurus's tail holds a ball of bone. It will try to hit the T. rex with that. Will the ankylosaurus be able to fight off the T. rex? Or will the giant predator be able to kill this tough, plant-eating dinosaur?

DINO STATS

T. Rex

Weight: 8.8 tons (8 t)
Length: 41 feet (12.5 m)
Main weapons: Speed, large teeth, crushing bite

Ankylosaurus

Weight: 8.8 tons (8 t)
Length: 33 feet (10 m)
Main weapons: Armored skin, bone spikes, tail club

T. REX VS. ANKYLOSAURUS

A huge asteroid wiped out the dinosaurs.

Both the T. rex and ankylosaurus lived in what is now North America. They were two of the last kinds of dinosaurs to ever live. The last dinosaurs died about sixty-six million years ago. There were no humans around then to see what happened. Scientists have figured out that the dinosaurs were all killed when a huge asteroid hit Earth.

Everything we know about ankylosauruses and T. rexes comes from fossils. Fossils are body parts, such as bones or teeth, that have turned to solid rock. Scientists look at the shapes and sizes of fossils to learn how different dinosaurs lived. They have discovered that the T. rex and the ankylosaurus were two of the toughest animals ever!

Size and Weight

A T. rex's tail was about 20 feet (6 m) long. That made it twice as long as an ankylosaurus tail. The T. rex was also much taller. An ankylosaurus was as tall as an adult woman. A T. rex was twice the height of an adult man.

The T. rex was one of the largest and fiercest predators to ever live.

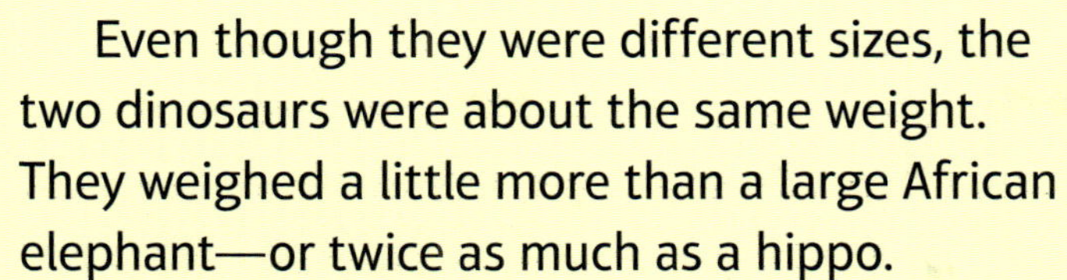

Even though they were different sizes, the two dinosaurs were about the same weight. They weighed a little more than a large African elephant—or twice as much as a hippo.

The ankylosaurus was very heavy because of its thick bones and armor.

The ankylosaurus belonged to a group of dinosaurs called the thyreophorans. This name means "shield carrier." All thyreophorans had bone plates to protect them. Another member of this group was the stegosaurus.

Fast and Slow

A T. rex's arms were very short, with only two fingers and claws. It walked on its two back legs. The T. rex was big, but it could move around and chase prey. It could run at about 12 miles (20 km) per hour. That is about as fast as an adult person runs.

The smaller ankylosaurus was covered in armor. Its body was very wide and heavy. This meant it was much slower than a T. rex. An ankylosaurus always walked on four legs. It had a top running speed of just 3 miles (5 km) per hour. That is about as fast as an adult walks!

A T. rex stood on its prey with its back feet to hold it still. It could then rip off chunks of meat with its teeth.

Bites and Teeth

The T. rex had the strongest bite of any animal ever. It was twelve times stronger than a grizzly bear's bite. A T. rex could crush its prey's bones in its jaws. The T. rex needed strong teeth that would not break. It had sixty banana-shaped teeth. Each one was 8 inches (20 cm) long. That is about as long as an adult man's hand.

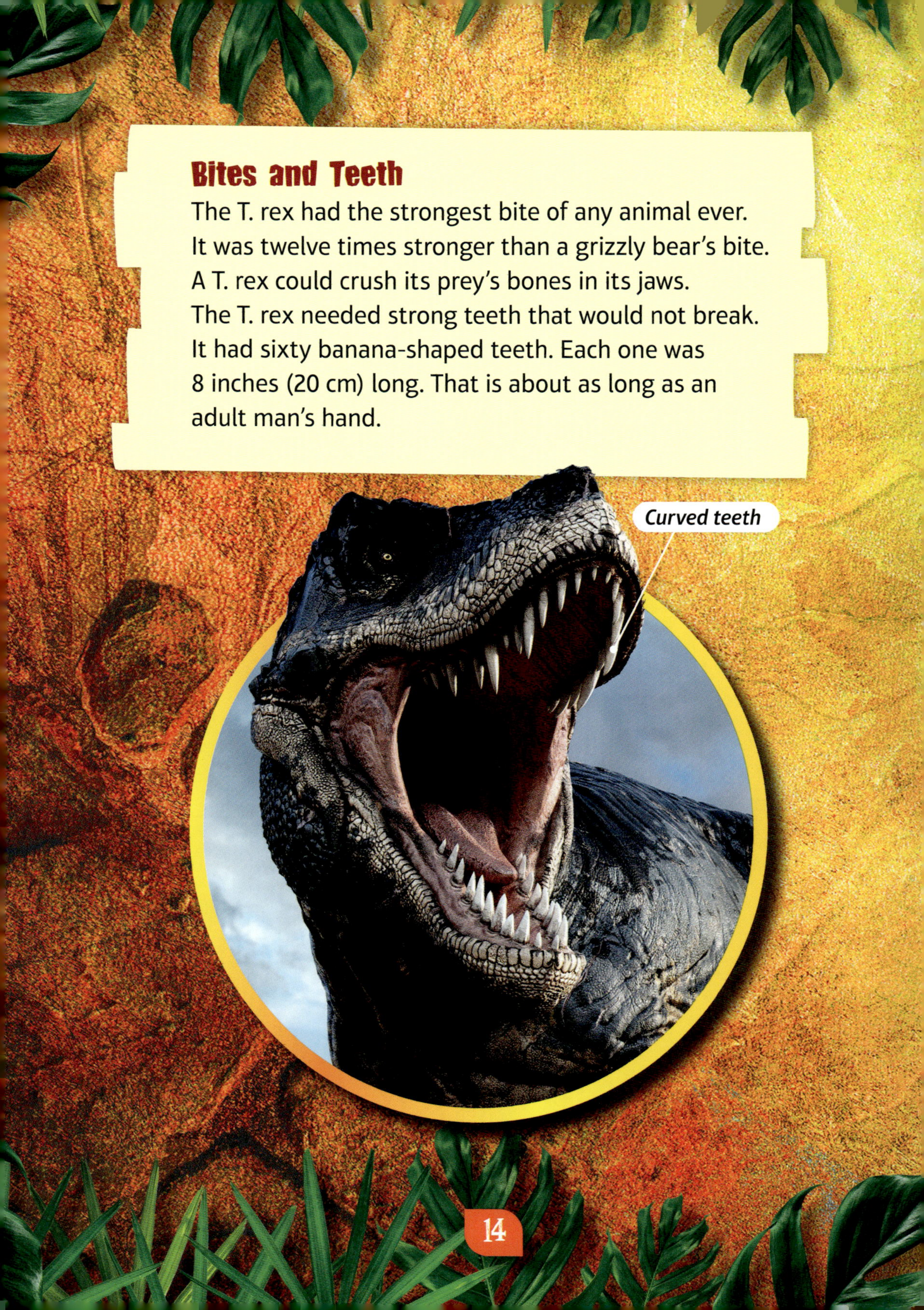

An ankylosaurus's mouth was more than 2 feet (60 cm) wide! However, its teeth were very small. They were used for grinding up leaves. The ankylosaurus also had a strong tongue, which helped mash up food.

An ankylosaurus needed to eat about 130 pounds (60 kg) of food every day. That is about as much as an African elephant eats today.

Looking at Skin

The name *ankylosaurus* means "fused lizard." That name comes from the plates of bone underneath the dinosaur's skin. The plates covered most of the body, especially the head and back. An ankylosaurus even had these armor plates in its eyelids!

An ankylosaurus was protected by its bone armor.

Birds are related to feathered dinosaurs similar to the T. rex.

Scientists are less sure about the skin of a T. rex. Many of its relatives had feathers covering the skin. It is possible that baby T. rexes had feathers. Fossils of T. rex skin show that the adults had skin covered in tough scales.

The T. rex's arms were too short to reach its mouth. They probably used their arms to grab prey as the T. rex bit down.

Different Senses

An ankylosaurus had a very good sense of smell. This helped it find the freshest plants to eat. However, it was probably short-sighted. That meant it could not see things far away very clearly.

An ankylosaurus spent all day sniffing out the freshest leaves to eat.

There were long tubes inside the nose of an ankylosaurus. These were not for smelling, but for keeping the animal cool. Extra body heat passed through the nose and was breathed out.

A T. rex had very powerful senses of smell and sight.

A T. rex also had a very good sense of smell for sniffing food. And it had excellent vision. It could see thirteen times better than a person. A T. rex's eye was the size of a grapefruit. They could make out objects 3.5 miles (6 km) away. A person can only see as far as about 1 mile (1.6 km) away. A T. rex saw in color and could pick up ultraviolet light. This light is invisible to our eyes.

Living Alone

It is hard to know if the T. rex or ankylosaurus lived in families or other groups. Young ankylosauruses may have lived in small herds, but the adults probably lived alone. That is how big plant-eaters such as rhinos live today.

A pair of ankylosauruses grazing together

When new T. rex fossils are found, they are normally of just one animal. That suggests that T. rexes lived by themselves as well. Scientists think they were often scavengers that ate animals that were already dead. Some other kinds of hunting dinosaurs probably lived in packs that attacked prey as a team.

Fossil hunters dig up a T. rex skeleton.

There are fossil footprints that show three T. rexes meeting up. No one knows if they were just passing each other, fighting, or were part of a group.

A T. rex could not stand up without using its tail for balance.

Tale of Tails

The tails of a T. rex and an ankylosaurus were both very different. The tail was used to help them balance. When the T. rex was walking or running, it leaned its head forward. The tail lifted up behind the body to balance the front so the dinosaur did not fall over. This meant the T. rex's tail had to be quite stiff.

An ankylosaurus's tail was its main weapon. It had a heavy club made of bone on the end. Ankylosauruses used this club in fights over mates. Their armor protected them from serious injuries. However, if another kind of dinosaur was hit by this club, it could crack its bones.

An ankylosaurus swings the heavy bone ball on the end of its tail.

CHOOSE YOUR WINNER

A T. rex has ambushed an ankylosaurus while it was grazing in a forest. The blood-thirsty dinosaur stomps over to the smaller plant-eater. It leans down with its enormous head and clamps its mouth around the ankylosaurus's neck. In most animals the neck is a weak point. A T. rex's bite would crush it!

But the T. rex's attack is not going to plan. The ankylosaurus's armor is too thick even for the T. rex's huge teeth. The ankylosaurus has spiked horns that stick out from behind the head. It uses these to jab the T. rex's face until it lets go.

The full name for a T. rex is Tyrannosaurus rex. That means "King of the Tyrant Lizards." A tyrant is a very cruel leader.

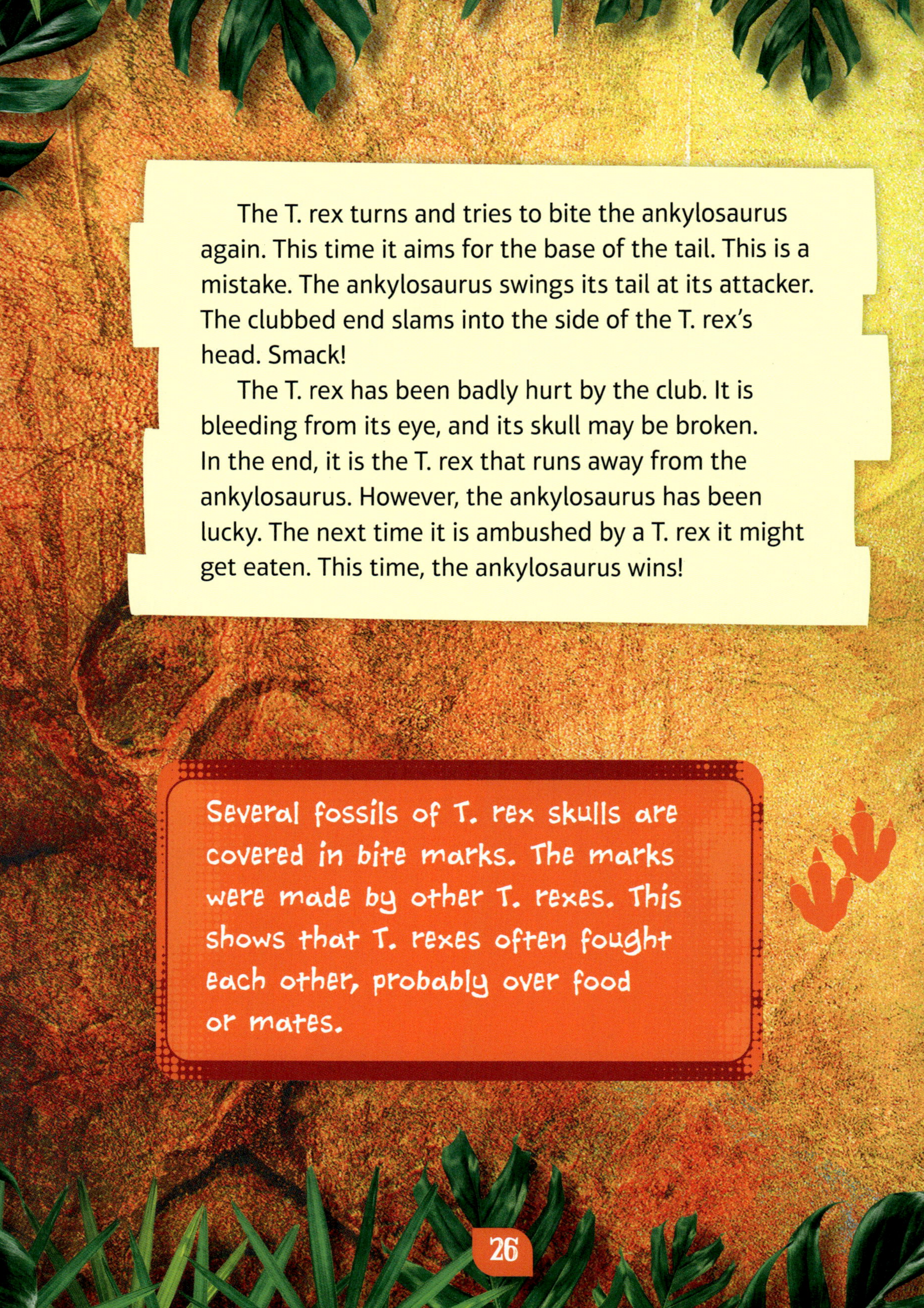

The T. rex turns and tries to bite the ankylosaurus again. This time it aims for the base of the tail. This is a mistake. The ankylosaurus swings its tail at its attacker. The clubbed end slams into the side of the T. rex's head. Smack!

The T. rex has been badly hurt by the club. It is bleeding from its eye, and its skull may be broken. In the end, it is the T. rex that runs away from the ankylosaurus. However, the ankylosaurus has been lucky. The next time it is ambushed by a T. rex it might get eaten. This time, the ankylosaurus wins!

Several fossils of T. rex skulls are covered in bite marks. The marks were made by other T. rexes. This shows that T. rexes often fought each other, probably over food or mates.

The ankylosaurus wins!

DINO DUEL

T. Rex

- Curved teeth
- Crushing bite
- Excellent vision
- Clawed feet

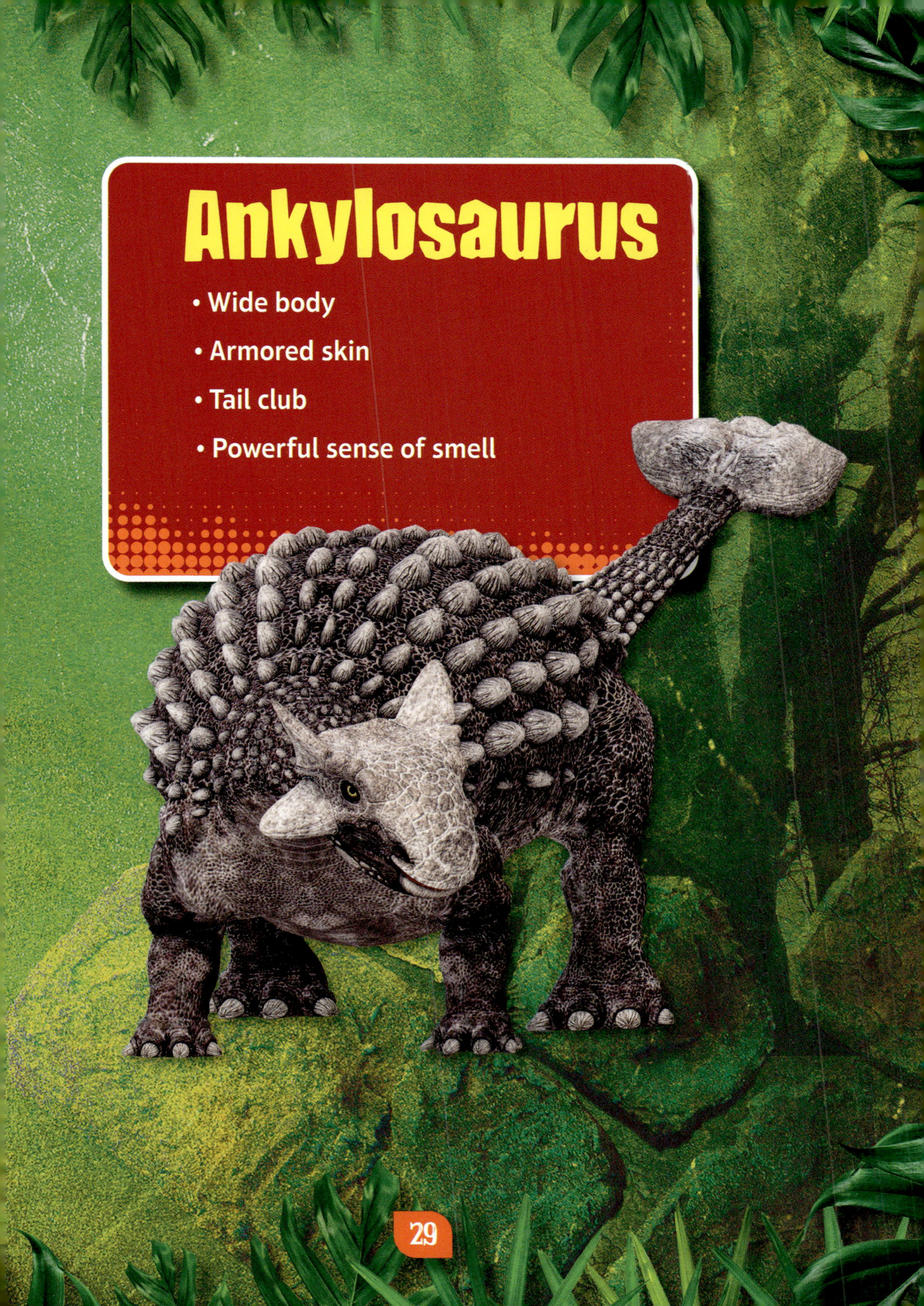

Ankylosaurus

- Wide body
- Armored skin
- Tail club
- Powerful sense of smell

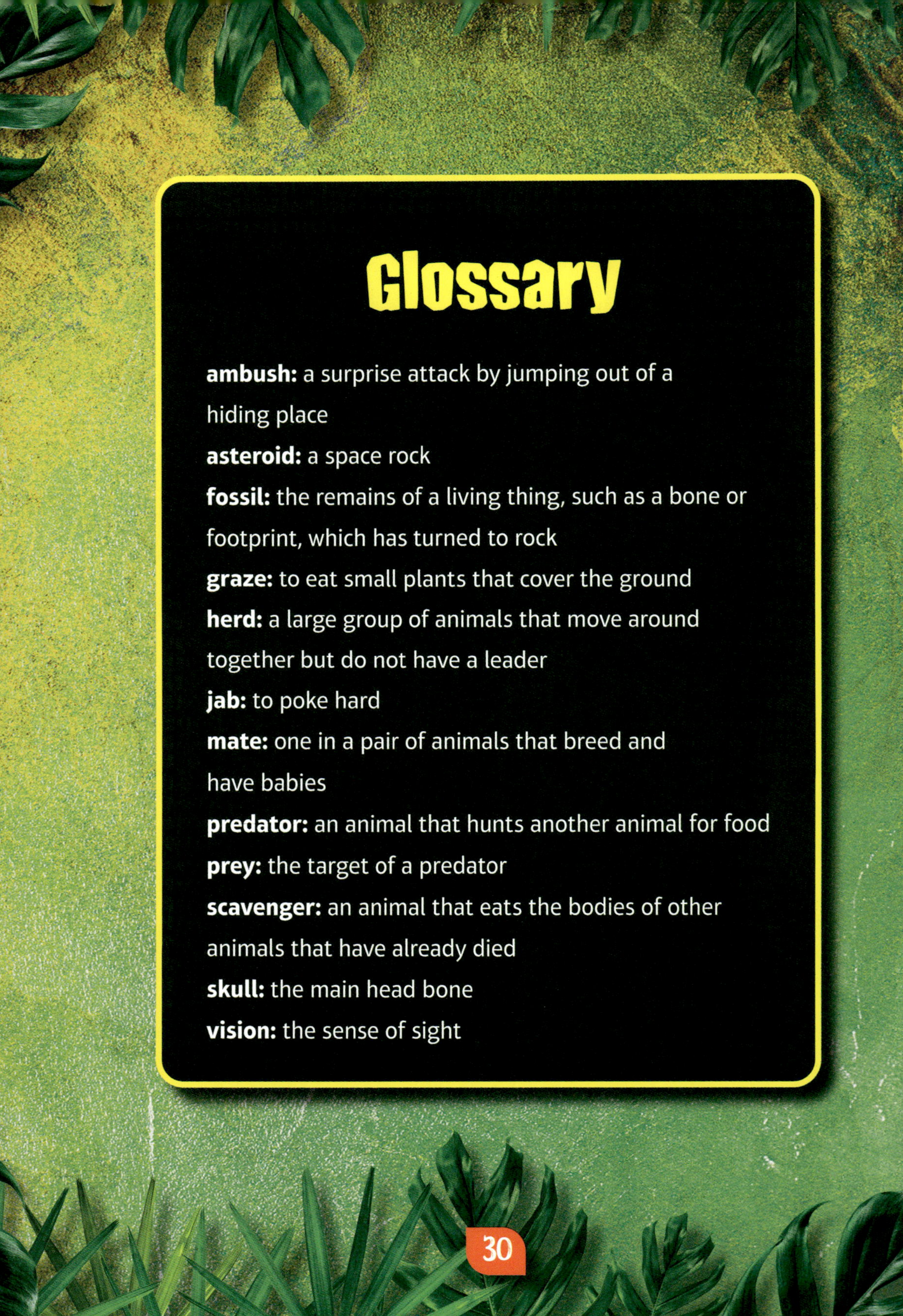

Glossary

ambush: a surprise attack by jumping out of a hiding place

asteroid: a space rock

fossil: the remains of a living thing, such as a bone or footprint, which has turned to rock

graze: to eat small plants that cover the ground

herd: a large group of animals that move around together but do not have a leader

jab: to poke hard

mate: one in a pair of animals that breed and have babies

predator: an animal that hunts another animal for food

prey: the target of a predator

scavenger: an animal that eats the bodies of other animals that have already died

skull: the main head bone

vision: the sense of sight

Britannica Kids: Tyrannosaurus Rex
https://kids.britannica.com/kids/article/Tyrannosaurus-Rex/353881

Chinsamy-Turan, Anusuya. *Dinosaurs and Other Prehistoric Life.* New York: Dorling Kindersley Publishing, 2021.

Eason, Sarah. *Bones in the Cliff: T. Rex Discovery.* Minneapolis: Bearport, 2022.

National Geographic Kids: Tyrannosaurus Rex
https://kids.nationalgeographic.com/animals/prehistoric/facts/tyrannosaurus-rex

Natural History Museum: Ankylosaurus
https://www.nhm.ac.uk/discover/dino-directory/ankylosaurus.html

Radley, Gail, *Ankylosaurus.* Mankato, MN: Black Rabbit Books, 2021.

Index

armor plate, 6, 11, 16

bite, 6–7, 14, 24, 26

claw, 12
club, 7, 23, 26

footprint, 21

horn, 25

speed, 13

tail, 7, 10, 22–23, 26
teeth, 5, 7, 9, 13–15, 25

Photo Acknowledgments

Image credits: Liidia/Shutterstock, p. 1; Orlando Florin Rosu/Dreamstime.com, pp. 4, 23; Daniel Eskridge/Shutterstock, pp. 5, 20, 24–25; Orla/Shutterstock, pp. 6, 10, 15, 18; Matis 75/Shutterstock, pp. 7a; Innakote/Shutterstock, p. 7b; serpeblu/Shutterstock, p. 8; Gary Todd/Wikimedia Commons, p. 9; Alberto Andrei Rosu/Shutterstock, p. 11; 1 2 3D illustration/Shutterstock, p. 12; Sebastian Kaulitzki/Shutterstock, p. 13; Warpaint/Shutterstock, pp. 14, 22, 28; Daniel Eskridge/Dreamstime.com, pp. 16, 27; Durbed/Wikimedia Commons, p. 17; Mracka/Dreamstime.com, p. 19; Rafael Trafaniuc/Shutterstock, p. 21; Ralf Juergen Kraft/Shutterstock, p. 29. Design elements: Kompaniets Taras/Shutterstock; Chaiyapong/Shutterstock.

Cover: Liidia/Shutterstock; Kompaniets Taras/Shutterstock; Chaiyapong/Shutterstock; Warpaint/Shutterstock (top); Daniel Eskridge/Shutterstock (bottom).